YUCK!
ICKY, STICKY, GROSS STUFF IN YOUR GARDEN

by Pam Rosenberg
illustrated by Beatriz Helena Ramos

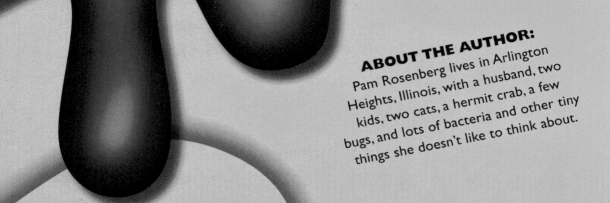

ABOUT THE AUTHOR:

Pam Rosenberg lives in Arlington Heights, Illinois, with a husband, two kids, two cats, a hermit crab, a few bugs, and lots of bacteria and other tiny things she doesn't like to think about.

ABOUT THE ILLUSTRATOR:

Beatriz Helena Ramos is an artist from Venezuela who lives and plays in NYC. She works from her animation studio, Dancing Diablo, where she directs animated spots. Beatriz has illustrated a dozen books and she particularly loves gross stories.

The Child's World®

Published in the United States of America
by The Child's World®
1980 Lookout Drive • Mankato, MN 56003-1705
800-599-READ • www.childsworld.com

Acknowledgments
The Child's World®: Mary Berendes, Publishing Director
The Design Lab: Kathleen Petelinsek, Design and Page Production
Red Line Editorial: Editing

Photo Credits
iStockphoto.com/Cathy Keifer: 9; iStockphoto.com/gremlin: cover; Scott Camazine/Alamy: 15

Library of Congress Cataloging-in-Publication Data
Rosenberg, Pam.
 Yuck! icky, sticky, gross stuff in your garden / by Pam Rosenberg ;
illustrated by Beatriz Helena Ramos.
     p. cm. —(Icky, sticky, gross-out books)
 ISBN-13: 978-1-59296-896-1 (library bound : alk. paper)
 ISBN-10: 1-59296-896-1 (library bound : alk. paper)
 1. Garden animals—Juvenile literature. 2. Soil animals—Juvenile literature.
I. Ramos, Beatriz Helena, ill. II. Title.
 QL119.R676 2007
 577.5'54—dc22   2007000404

CONTENTS

IT'S A BEAUTIFUL DAY TO BE OUTSIDE.

The sun is shining. A warm breeze is blowing. It's a great day to look at flowers and other plants. But don't look too close— what you find there may just send you running back inside for cover.

JOIN ME IN THE GARDEN— IF YOU'RE BRAVE ENOUGH!

Don't Eat the Dirt!

Any good gardener knows that you need good soil for growing healthy plants. But the plants you see growing out of the soil aren't the only living things in it. There are **billions** organisms that make their home in soil. Many, such as bacteria, can only be seen with a microscope. **One shovelful of soil may contain more living things than the number of people that have ever lived on Earth!**

Soil amoebas look like little blobs under a microscope. They use their tentacles to move and grab food. They surround food with their tentacles and bring it into their bodies, no chewing required! **Amoebas eat bacteria, thousands of them a day.**

Thousands of different bacteria live in the soil. Most of them break down dead plants and animals and return their **nutrients** to the soil. This helps keep soil **fertile**, or good for growing plants. **Bacteria have a simple way of reproducing—they just split themselves in two.** Some of them split in two **as often as every 20 minutes.** Imagine what would happen if people could do that!

Scientists think there are about **5 billion bacteria in one teaspoon of soil.** (Now you know why this section is called Don't Eat the Dirt!)

Earthworms also keep soil fertile. They eat dead things in the ground and swallow soil as they burrow through it. The bacteria in the soil they eat grow very well in earthworm guts. **When the earthworm poops, it puts more bacteria into the soil than it took out when it ate.**

How much soil do you think all of the earthworms living in an area the size of a football field eat in a year? If you said **4 tons,** you are correct!

South Africa was home to the **largest earthworm** every found. This monster worm was **22 feet** (6.7 meters) long!

Earthworms are packed with protein. They are a favorite food of birds. Bet you didn't know that **some people eat worms,** too! Fried worms, anyone?

worms worms worms

Pesty Garden Visitors

SLIMY SLUGS

What's that soft, slimy thing leaving a trail of goo behind it? A slug! These little guys are related to snails and look a lot like snails without their shells. They slide along on a single foot, leaving a trail of slime behind them. They like to eat plants. If you have a beautiful plant that suddenly looks like a piece of Swiss cheese, your garden may have been invaded by slugs.

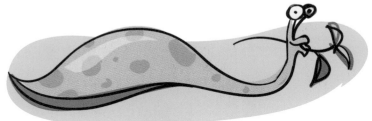

To make matters worse, slugs don't need a mate to reproduce. Each slug has male and female reproductive parts! A slug lays two to three dozen eggs at a time, and they lay eggs several times a year. So if you find one slug and don't get rid of it, don't be surprised to find lots of slugs in your garden a few months later!

LOCUSTS

Did you ever read that story in the Bible about God sending a plague of locusts down on Egypt? Maybe you wondered what the big deal was. Why should anyone be scared of locusts? Well, if you were a farmer with a nice big garden (otherwise known as a farm) you'd be very afraid. **These hoppers are very hungry bugs. They eat their own weight in food every day, and they've been known to travel in groups of 40 million or more.**

PLANT LICE

Aphids are tiny little pests that can do some serious damage to plants of all kinds. Their poop is called *honeydew* and ants, bees, and wasps collect it for food!

If you don't like to use chemicals to kill pests in your garden, you can help control the aphids by bringing in some ladybugs. Those cute little black-spotted red bugs love to eat aphids. **One ladybug can eat fifty aphids in a day!**

PRAYING MANTIS

The **praying mantis** is a scary-looking insect. They can be **3 to 5 inches** (8 to 13 centimeters) long! But you may not want to get rid of these scary-looking visitors. It doesn't eat your plants. Instead, it **eats the bugs that eat your plants.** Some of its favorite foods are beetles, grasshoppers, and other insects. It also eats bigger animals like mice and tree frogs.

How does the praying mantis catch its prey? It uses its front legs which are strong and covered with spines. Most victims can't escape. **The praying mantis starts eating its victims while they are still alive.**

Like most insects, praying mantises lay eggs. When the young hatch, they are hungry. **What is a baby praying mantis's first meal?** Lots of times it eats one of its **newly hatched brothers or sisters!**

The Pollinators

Many flowering plants need the help of animals, such as insects and birds, to reproduce. These animals carry **pollen** from one plant to another plant of the same kind. This transfer of pollen is necessary for the plants to produce seeds. **Here are some grossly interesting facts about some plant pollinators.**

BEES

Do you like honey? Think it is sweet, sticky, and yummy? Next time you're dipping your chicken nuggets in some honey, think about this: **Honey is bee barf!** Yes—when bees drink the **nectar** from flowers, it is turned into honey in their bodies. Back at their nest, they spit it back up and store it in their honeycombs.

HONEY

Normally, bees are welcome visitors to a garden. They go from plant to plant in search of the nectar to make honey. In the process, they pollinate the plants and help them reproduce. But **killer bees,** or Africanized honey bees, are a different story. If their nest is disturbed, they **will attack in great numbers.** They will chase a person for a quarter of a mile (.4 km) or more!

If that isn't enough to gross you out, think about this. **Killer bees sting in swarms.** That means, you'd be chased by more than one bee—there would be a whole crowd of them after you. What should you do? Run away as quick as you can and get into a car or a house and away from the bees!

BEETLES

Dung beetles are named for the food they eat—poop! Yes, "dung" is another word for "manure," which is just a fancy name for poop. Many dung beetles roll the manure into balls and save them for a day when they can't find a pile of poop to eat. Some even roll themselves inside a ball of poop. Then they lay their eggs inside the ball of poop and crawl out. When the eggs hatch they have a delicious ball of poop to eat for their first meal!

One kind of flower found on the island of Borneo **mimics the smell of poop** to attract dung beetles to its flowers. The beetles arrive thinking they are in for a meal. They leave the plant covered with pollen but without a meal.

FLIES

Do you like chocolate? That tasty treat is made from cocoa and other ingredients. The cocoa comes from cocoa trees. The flowers of the **cocoa tree are pollinated by tiny flies called midges.** Midges are attracted to the smell of fungus and the cocoa flowers give off a scent that smells like mushrooms. Think about that next time you are enjoying the delicious taste of chocolate!

If you are enjoying a picnic outside, you might want to keep the flies away from your food. **Flies squirt a liquid out of their stomachs onto their food.** The liquid **dissolves** the food and the fly sucks up the liquid. Don't think that's too gross? Then think about this. Flies really like garbage and animal poop. And their feet are sticky. **That fly standing on top of your potato salad may have just flown over after snacking on the pile of dog poop** in your neighbor's backyard!

BUTTERFLIES

Butterflies spend much of their time flying from flower to flower drinking nectar. But did you know that many of these pretty insects also **feed on** some not-so-pretty things such as **rotting** fruit, the fluids in the bodies of **dead** animals, and **mud** puddles?

You may know that butterflies have a really long tongue, called a **proboscis** (pruh-BAH-siss), which rolls up when they aren't using it to drink. But did you know that, unlike people, **they don't use their tongues for tasting?** Instead, **they use their feet.** Try not to think about that the next time you take off your socks and shoes!

Monarch butterflies lay their eggs on milkweed plants. Milkweed is a **poisonous plant,** but monarch caterpillars can eat it without getting sick. The caterpillars feast on the leaves as they grow and the poison in the milkweed stays in their bodies. If an animal eats a monarch butterfly it gets very sick, but usually doesn't die. Birds and other animals that eat butterflies quickly learn not to eat monarch butterflies.

Eeewww! What's That on My Plant's Leaf?

If you ever see something on a **leaf in your garden that looks like bird poop,** take a closer look. It just might be a **swallowtail caterpillar.** These little guys hold their black-and-white bodies in the shape of a bird dropping and sit motionless on a leaf. This clever disguise keeps other animals from eating them—after all, who wants to eat poop?

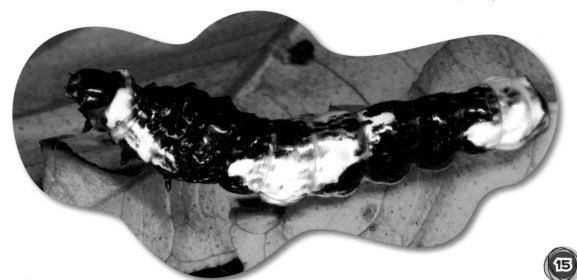

That cute, fuzzy caterpillar crawling on your plant may be full of other bugs. **One kind of wasp injects its eggs into the body of a caterpillar** or other host bug. As the eggs develop into baby wasps, **they feed on the caterpillar.** Then the wasps cover the body of their host with lots of tiny white COCOONS. They rest there for five or ten days while they develop into adult wasps. **When they are fully-grown, the wasps fly out of the body of the dead caterpillar.**

Oh, and by the way, you may not want to pick up a **cute, fuzzy caterpillar.** Some of these little guys **have stingers.** Pick one up and you may end up with a very itchy, painful hand!

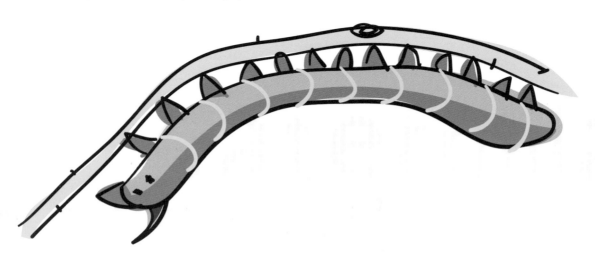

Ants In the Garden

Did you know that some kinds of ants create gardens of their own? Leaf cutter ants grow **fungus for food.** They cut out discs from leaves and bring them back to the nest. Then they cut the leaves into little pieces, **mix them with ant spit,** and put this leaf paste in their gardens. They plant some bits of fungus in the leaf paste and worker ants act as the gardeners and harvest the fungus to feed to baby ants and other adults.

Honey ants have a special way of storing *honeydew*. **Honeydew is the sweet liquid poop** of small bugs called aphids. **Ants gather honeydew for food.** One ant, called the **replete**, is used as the storage container for the honeydew. The other workers feed the replete until its abdomen is expanded to several times its normal size. The replete hangs from the ceiling of the ant colony until the ants need the honeydew for food. Then it **regurgitates** (ree-GUR-juh-tayt—a fancy word for pukes!) the honeydew for the other ants to eat.

Think it's gross that the ants eat something the replete throws up? Maybe not as gross as the fact that people in the parts of the world where honey ants live like to **eat the honey ants as a sweet treat.** Yummy!

Meat-eating Plants

If you like unusual plants in your garden, you might try to grow **pitcher plants.** They have a part that looks like a cup or pitcher. Insects are attracted to the plant and if they are unlucky enough to enter the pitcher, they are **eaten by the plant!**

Most pitcher plants eat insects, but some eat larger animals such as frogs. Some frogs like to sit in pitcher plants and catch the insects that are attracted to the plants. But if a frog is unlucky enough to jump into a pitcher that eats frogs, it will be digested. **All that is left when the plant is done digesting the frog is the skin of the frog's hands!**

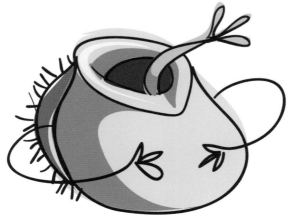

Venus flytrap plants have leaves with short, stiff hairs. If an insect, such as a fly, lands on the leaf and touches one of these trigger hairs, the two sides of the leaf close up. **Then the plant's juices dissolve the insect's soft parts. The only thing that doesn't get digested is the bug's hard outer shell.** When digestion is complete—usually in five to twelve days—the leaves open back up. The dried up shell that wasn't digested is either blown off the leaf by wind or washed away by rain.

What's That Smell?

How would you like to find a plant 6 feet (1.8 meters) tall that stinks like rotting flesh growing in your garden? The titan arum is the name of this monster of a plant, but it is often called the corpse flower because of its awful smell. This is definitely not a flower scent you'd want in your perfume!

Ready to go inside now, where it's safe? You'd better hope that none of the **bacteria** and **amoebas** are stuck to your shoes when you come inside. Oh, and wait—is that a fly that just flew in the door? Maybe the garden isn't so gross, after all!

GLOSSARY

amoebas (uh-MEE-buhs) Amoebas are single-celled microscopic organisms. Amoebas that live is soil eat bacteria.

bacteria (bak-TEER-ee-uh) Bacteria are microscopic living things. Thousands of different kinds of bacteria live in soil.

chemicals (KEM-uh-kuhlz) Chemicals are substances that are used in chemistry, the study of what substances are made of and how they react with one another. Some chemicals can be used to kill pests in gardens.

cocoons (kuh-KOONS) Cocoons are coverings made by some insects to protect themselves or their eggs. Some wasps spin themselves into cocoons on the body of a caterpillar.

corpse (KORPS) A corpse is a dead body. The titan arum is known as the corpse plant because it smells like dead, rotting flesh.

digested (dye-JEST-ed) Food that is digested is broken down so that it can be absorbed and used by the body. A frog that lands on a certain kind of pitcher plant will be digested by the plant.

dissolves (di-ZOLVS) Something that dissolves seems to disappear when it is mixed with water or some other liquid. Flies squirt a liquid onto their food that dissolves the food.

fertile (FUR-tuhl) Something that is fertile is good for growing things. Fertile soil is good for growing crops.

mimics (MIM-iks) Something that mimics imitates the characteristics of something else. One kind of flower found on the island of Borneo mimics the smell of poop to attract dung beetles to its flowers.

nectar (NEK-tur) Nectar is a sweet liquid produced by flowers and used by bees to make honey.

nutrients (NOO-tree-uhnts) Nutrients are things that supply nourishment to a living organism. Bacteria break down dead plants and animals and return their nutrients to the soil.

organisms (OR-guh-niz-uhms) Organisms are living plants or animals. Billions of organisms make their homes in soil.

plague (PLAYG) A plague is a very serious disease or terrible event that affects many people. In the Bible, God sent a plague of locusts down on Egypt.

pollen (POL-uhn) Pollen is tiny yellow grains that are the male cells of flowering plants. The transfer of pollen from one plant to another is necessary for plants to produce seeds.

proboscis (pruh-BAH-siss) A proboscis is a long flexible tube used by an insect to take in fluids. Butterflies have a long tongue-like proboscis which rolls up when they aren't using it to drink.

protein (PROH-teen) Protein is a substance that is found in living plant and animal cells. Earthworms are packed with protein.

regurgitates (ree-GUR-juh-tates) When an animal regurgitates, it brings food from its stomach back into its mouth. An ant known as a replete regurgitates honeydew for other ants in the colony to eat.

replete (rih-PLEET) A replete is an ant that is used as a storage container for the honeydew collected by ants in a colony. The replete hangs from the ceiling of the ant colony until the ants need the honeydew for food.

reproducing (ree-pruh-DOOSS-ing) When living things are reproducing, they are producing offspring. Bacteria have a simple way of reproducing, they simply split themselves in two.

tentacles (TEN-tuh-kuhls) Tentacles are long, flexible limbs found on some living things. Amoebas use their tentacles to move and grab food.

FOR MORE INFORMATION

Bull, Jane. *The Gardening Book: 50 Green-Fingered and Growing Activities.* London: Dorling Kindersley, 2003

Kudlinski, Kathleen V., and Jerome Wexler. *Venus Flytraps.* Minneapolis, MN: Lerner Publications, 1998.

McLaughlin, Molly. *Earthworms, Dirt, and Rotten Leaves: An Exploration in Ecology.* New York: Atheneum, 1986.

INDEX